I0504762

The Other Side Of Wall Street System

When your broker trades your money (and even when you do your own day trading), you are trading the "retail" side of the market. You are buying an underlying asset and hoping the market moves in your predicted direction. Only then can you profit. Since the market always does one of 3 things – goes up, goes down or stays flat – you have only a 1 out of 3 probability of profiting. This is gambling. In any type of gambling, ultimately the House wins. It's time to change the odds.

We teach you the trading secret that the brokerage firms use to trade their own money – Non-directional Trading. By abandoning everything you were taught about trading, you can learn the systematic strategy to profit no matter if the market goes up, goes down, or stays flat. "How could that possibly work?" you ask.

3 Essential Tenets

1. Leverage Non-Directional Trading – Profit no matter if the market goes, goes down or stays flat.

2. Master your Trading Psychology – How and what you think is what makes you a successful trader.

3. Achieve Financial Freedom – Take your financial future in your own hands. Trade your own account. Reduce Risk. Increase Profit.

https://www.theothersideofwallstreet.org

TABLE OF CONTENTS

FORWARD

The nature of the market is purposeful chaos. This is so because the market is the aggregate actions of thousands of people, therefore it cannot be trusted. It will change on you at the flick of a finger, void plans, erase profits, render prior knowledge obsolete or even render you penniless if you don't play your cards right. Patterns change, so don't just rely on it totally. One day it could be favorable for you, but that can change the next day, even the next hour or so. So, this is a basic introduction to a trading mindset, and this can help you be on your way to more profitable gains and calculated risks.

CHAPTER 1

A BASIC INTRODUCTION TO REPROGRAMING THE TRADERS MINDSET

Many people talk about the wonders of trading and how it can be best approached but knowing how to establish and identify your entry signals can mean a lot to setting the right path to trading, therefore, a basic introduction to trading must be in order.

The primary goal to trading is for profit, since the penultimate goal for it is to sell for a profit. But do take note that trading is like gambling, where one cannot determine or tell what exact market forces are at play and what it can ultimately do to spoil your trading choices.

Self-determination is another key to your trading success. No one will tell you what to do next, you must plan for yourself, especially since there are no hard and fast rules for this career.

Other people may tell you what to do, and they could be right for a time, but do try to consider that the point is that the market fluctuates, and trading is about watching the market, analyzing it, and acting on your own.

Understand and manager your opportunities and risks.

All those people grabbing opportunities mean that the really good ones go away.

The random opportunity that most likely pops up in a trader's life is a crisis in supply. Something has interrupted the normal flow of supply and demand, dramatically raising the price and this is a temporary chance.

Others will also be jumping on opportunities the same as you do. These may be the regular suppliers, those with surplus stock or another trader with a source elsewhere.

Wisely judge the risk and make your move.

Gambling to win means not letting the house make the rules. The difference between luck and success lies in the amount of risk managed. Sometimes you could get lucky and at other times not, so risk analysis and management lie at the heart of any method that can be termed reliable.

Setbacks happen and this is a risk in trading, where there are casualties and losses. Play at the stakes and risk levels you can afford, don't lay down all your cards and have nothing left to pick up on. Make every effort to know the market. This will help a lot in determining how you could establish the ins and outs of the market you are in.

Every trader needs to know his territory, and those specific markets he or she is interested in

Trading is a world of compound interest, challenges and opportunities. One can invest in buying and selling more items in a single item market, you can pick up when you feel there is a slack on one item, or you can diversify into other types of items.

The nature of the market is purposeful chaos. This is so because the market is the aggregate actions of thousands of people, therefore it cannot be trusted. It will change on you at the flick of a finger, void plans, erase profits, render prior knowledge obsolete or even render you penniless if you don't play your cards right. Patterns change, so don't just rely on it totally. As what the previous point indicates, one day it could be favorable for you, but that can change the next day, even the next hour or so. So, this is a basic introduction to a trading mindset, and this can help you be on your way to more profitable gains and calculated risks.

CHAPTER 2

ATTITUDE AND YOUR TRADING MINDSET

Traders own their business and set its direction and as leaders they must know how to run their business which is essential to their success, frankly, attitude and your trading mindset can spell your success or failure.

Statistically, 90% of traders lose money.

The trading mindset challenge is how to face up to the challenge of making it among the 10% who make it big in trading.

One way is to understand leadership principles and see how you are applying them to your own trading business.

First, you must know why you are in the trading business, what attracted you to it, what were your motivations, and will you be seriously focusing your undivided attention to making it succeed?

Many say that it is money, excitement, challenge, power and a lot of other things.

Imagine you got all of the things you wanted to get out of your trading business:

Setting your own trading mindset will help you get along the way, especially when your attitude comes into the picture.

What is your degree of discipline, how you tend to react to certain conditions and circumstances, how focused are you towards reaching your goals, do you give up easily, etc.?

Managing your energy, time and effort is one sure way to establish a habit and creating a discipline that you hope to use in shaping the path of your trading venture.

One good principle to follow is the 80/20 rule, where 20% of your efforts get 80% of your desired results.

You can focus your energy on the efforts that get you the results or let yourself get distracted. If you allow yourself to get distracted, however you will not produce the result that you want in the time frame that you want.

Perception is also another useful tool in establishing the right attitude for your trading mindset.

We face challenges and difficulties throughout our trading business, but this is just a normal fact of trading.

Question is, how do you deal with these setbacks?

If you consider your losses as being the cost of doing business and an overhead for your business, then it is easier to accept the fact and move on, taking into consideration that your loss is a way for you to learn from it and avoid it from occurring another time.

It is important to realize that it is about your perception and how you view it. Losing is not an option, it is a fact of life that one must deal with and how you perceive it will make you reshape your path towards your trading mindset.

Of course, fear has a way of making one reluctant about a certain decision but take advantage of the fear in making calculated risks and having other options if one trading decision does not work to your advantage.

Take ownership of your trading business, make your decisions work for you and not let others do it for you.

Trading is a stiff competitive market and a hard truth to it is that if there are winners, there definitely has to be losers, otherwise it cannot be considered a market.

Many of us put more value in others' opinions than our own and we tend to want to be safe rather than sorry and if something goes wrong, we have someone else to blame, as long as it is not us.

If we follow others, we do not have to take responsibility for our results. We can blame the advice, the markets or anything else, but the sign of true leadership and the ideal trading mindset is that you should not fear mistakes, but on how to handle the consequences and eventually move on.

One of the signs of great leaders is not that they do not make mistakes. It is that they handle the consequences and move on.

Remember that the most important thing to establishing a trading mindset is not only to make decisions, but also how to live with the consequences and how to take things in stride.

Your attitude and trading mindset, if done for the right reasons, conditions and goals, will definitely spell out your advantage over others.

CHAPTER 3

HOW TO STRENGTHEN YOUR TRADING MINDSET

To be able to succeed at trading, you must be fully aware of how to strengthen your trading mindset.

Trying your luck at trading is as good as trying your luck at a card game table in a casino, you take a gamble by placing your bet on what you consider your aces, try to establish a fallback position by managing your risks and how to play with your cards to make the most out of every possible gambling situation you are in, whether you win or lose.

Here are some common tips on how to strengthen your trading mindset.

Always take full responsibility for your trading decisions.

As a rule of thumb, most investors simply follow the crowd, but successful traders make up their own minds.

Although you should always be open to good advice from other experts, but the final and ultimate decision rests upon you and not with anybody else.

You can always try to focus on the opportunity to learn since there's plenty of it, but don't let it cloud your perspective or determine the choices you make.

Avoid the pitfalls of over-trading.

There are basically two types of over-trading - trading too often and trading too many shares or too large of a contract.

If you are trading too often, remind yourself that there's really no good reason to trade constantly, since extreme over-trading creates stress, produces high commissions but sometimes often leads to losses.

This is so because market forces do not last forever and time has shown various examples of the law of gravity in the trading market- that whatever comes up must go down.

Instead of grabbing every stock that comes along, make sure each trade setup meets the criteria of your trading plan, don't be too over cocky or too selfish.

To prevent trading too many shares, use a risk calculator to determine the appropriate position size before you click the enter button. It relieves stress to know that the amount at risk for each position you hold is safely proportioned to the size of your entire account, this is asset management at work.

Always go easy on yourself.

There's a tendency for traders who take responsibility for their actions to be tough on themselves.

After all, this gives credence to the saying that 'do not cry over spilled milk.'

This could be a good opportunity for some positive self-criticism, but don't slam yourself too hard or too often, since even the best traders make mistakes.

When you do, learn from them quickly and then let it go.

Avoid yelling at yourself, as self-inflicted psychological damage is tough to overcome, so it's best to avoid it entirely.

Always think like a winner.

Thinking like a winner turns you into a winner, since the sum of your thoughts has an interesting way of showing up in your life.

Thoughts are like muscles, the ones you use the most will grow to become the strongest. Work on the thoughts you want to develop and focus on them regularly, since it has the tendency to become action, action become habits, and habits determine results.

Always think of success and you are much closer to being on your way to success.

Lastly, take every effort to relax.

Even though trading is serious business, the best traders know how to laugh - especially at themselves.

Having fun and enjoying what you do is a very good motivator to give you focus on making money and earning it on trading.

So, know how to strengthen your trading mindset and be on your way to success.

CHAPTER 4

IMPORTANCE OF A CORRECT MINDSET IN TRADING

Having the right mindset is crucial in any kind of undertaking. And market trading is just one of the many examples of career paths where having a clear and focus state of mind can make the difference between disaster and success. Market trading is a risky business and not knowing more about the ins and outs makes success even more difficult to attain. But with the right attitude you get ahead. But what are the right attitudes in trading the market?

One of the more important tips in market trading is to keep your emotions at bay. There's no need to be emotional in a business where facts and numbers are all that matters. For example, you need not invest on stocks or trade stocks based on personal estimations. You based your decisions on known facts and calculated projections. You don't decide because you hope the stocks will improve or you hope your investment will be a good one. Stick with the facts.

Some will argue that instincts play a great deal in making decisions in market trading. To some extent it is indeed true. However, what will help you make the correct decisions are the instincts that you developed through your time and experience in the market. But instincts alone will not make you a great and successful trader.

If you have been experiencing a streak of good luck, it would be a good thing to learn to slow down since it is not really a good idea to keep relying on your instincts or good luck. You can become so full of yourself that you began to expand and trade on higher payoffs. This of course is a very common mistake and I'm telling you now that you need to avoid these kinds of decisions. Organize and develop your own set of trading rules to follow. This will allow you to step back if you find yourself in a pool of good luck and a string of successes.

Also look or cook your own recipe for success. Sure, a sound financial and educational base is needed to make a big start. Learning from others is imperative but relying on them is a mistake. And eventually, you need to accept loss. Remember that the best traders learn to accept loses and learn a lot when they do. Trading pushes you to your limit and your capabilities.

Thoughts become actions, actions become habits and habits give you the results.

Being pushed hard, traders need to maintain focus. A focused mind comes only with a clear head.

The best traders think like a winner. Thinking like a winner turns you into a winner. Identify the thoughts that you want to strengthen and focus on them regularly.

Even with pressures, you still need to go easy on yourself. There are traders who tend to be tough on themselves. A positive self-criticism is different from slapping your face too hard whenever you make mistakes. Learn from you mistakes and then let them go. Self-inflicted psychological damage is difficult to overcome, so it is best to avoid it totally.

Trading is a tough and serious business. But never be too hard on yourself. Relax. The best traders still know how to laugh, they even laugh on themselves. Having fun and relaxing your mind also keep your mind clear and focused. Having the correct trading mindset can give you immense results and at the same time have fun while you earn your bucks. Certainly, you deserve it.

CHAPTER 5

THE PSYCHOLOGY BEHIND THE TRADING MINDSET

The psychology behind the trading mindset deals a lot about how conditions govern a person's decisions with regards to commerce and trading.

Most experts agree that trading is generally categorized into three key areas, the mindset or psychology, money management and how a trader manages risk and the methods used for a particular trading system.

The mindset is, by far, the key area of the system that governs a trader's ability to control and drive trading market forces at play, especially how one would deal at a particular situation or circumstance

The key is that the mind drives everything you do in your life and trading is no exception.

Many people still think that at the onset of getting into trading, how come some end up successful, while some end up at the losing end.

Truth be told and many would agree, that when one asks what was responsible for them getting a good head start at trading, they would say that 'psychology' has a good deal of influence over it.

Essentially, it is the mental ability of managing losses and profits considering the good and bad periods in trading, as well as managing risk and not becoming too greedy, among others, are some of the major aspects that define 'trading psychology' or the trading mindset.

For one to be able to make good use of the trading mindset, it would be best to define how it works.

A trading mindset primarily deals with a person's character attributes, differentiating the strengths from weaknesses.

Are you a levelheaded person or highly emotional? This character attribute will make a good assessment of how a person deals with conditions and circumstances affecting one's decisions when it comes to trading.

Are you disciplined enough and willing to work hard to get the desired results? This attribute will spell how one deals or reacts to trading circumstances or situations that affect your trading forces.

However, to sum it all up, there will only be one overriding influence on trading success and that is attitude, which will eventually determine one's trading mindset.

Many experts will agree that attitude will determine if a trader's mindset is geared towards a profitable trading venture or method.

Attitude is by far more important than any of the other character attributes required for successful trading and it is more important than your market knowledge and your degree of skill, and this should be the ideal trading mindset that should govern one's trading choice.

Attitude is best described in a saying that goes 'It is not important what the market does to you, it is how you react to it that is important.'

For instance, it is not important when one is caught in a situation with the prospect of a losing trade, what is important is how one reacts to that situation and takes action to best help address it.

A good trading mindset is planning and knowing how to react to situations without letting a spur of the moment emotions cloud one's decision.

Essentially, a good trading mindset is to focus on the idea that successful trading is all about decision making, but because of money and inherent natural instincts, many people still associate their emotions from their decision-making process, which should not be the case.

So, it is best advised that to trade successfully, one must be aware of the psychology behind the trading mindset.

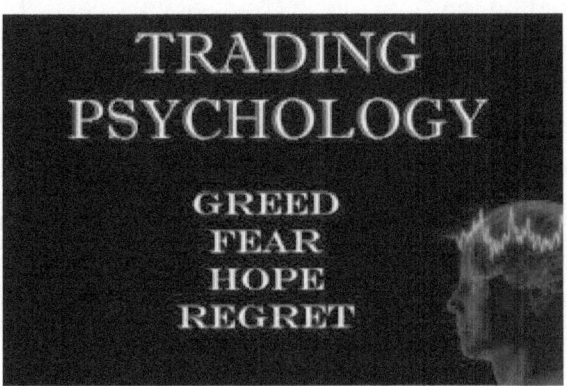

CHAPTER 6

TRADING MINDSET PSYCHOLOGY

There is a psychology behind trading. It is about the perceptions change that you go through once you are actively in the markets trading. Trading on a demo account seems easy, but once you have handled your first live trade, indecisiveness close in. understanding the trading psychology will help you get on to trading with the right mindset along with the following risk management.

Trading psychology and trading psychology issues are the predominant reasons why traders lose. It has been widely discussed in books and lectures that it has been a convenient excuse for losing. What is trading psychology? Trading psychology is an attitude or a reaction that a trader creates from existing personality traits. These personality traits may not be even related to trading or to market, but they surface from trading.

Common emotions brought about by this personality traits are fear and greed. Fear has a big effect on trading opportunities. Deals or trades may not be made because of fear or they may be closed prematurely before they reach or have a chance to profit. Meanwhile, greed will cause you to make trades which are too risky or too large while trying to accumulate gains.

Other emotions you have to check is failure and discipline. Failure is perfectly normal, but we should not let this get us down. Failure is expected and should make us better. While, discipline is about sticking to your methods and never deviating from it. There are traders who change their methods if they are having a winning and losing streak.

According to the trading mindset psychology, the reason traders lose is because they are not psychologically prepared for battle or for trade. There are traders that are not prepared to accept financial risk for something of which they have no control over the outcome. When traders experience consecutive losses, methods become replaced with a feeling of despair and hopelessness. Traders would have this feeling that it is impossible to do anything right, in this situation trading psychology is more crucial or critical than the trading method itself.

They say that trading is 90 percent psychological and 10 percent methodological. Even with a first class trading method, if the trader has no control over their emotions, it would be difficult for them to implement their trading method.

How to combat a troubled trading mindset?

You would have to make a trading plan and stick to it. This plan aims to have an honest assessment and understanding of the trader's action. You also need to define your trading methodology. You would have to master your emotions in order to seize the profits.

Self- confidence is an important attribute. If you lack confidence, then it would show in your results. Without confidence, you are not likely to trust and follow something that you have developed. Successful trading relies on decision making. Because of money and natural instincts, people cannot remove their emotions from their decision-making process. You also need to be disciplined with your decision making and focusing on the right areas. There are traders who tend to shed much of their energy thinking about the wrong things.

What the market does to you is not important. The market may lose or may profit today, but what is important is how you react to the market. Trading psychology may be made by some losing traders as their excuse, but bottom line is, a healthy trading mindset gives profitable results.

CHAPTER 7

TRADING PSYCHOLOGY- A LOSING AND SUCCESSFUL TRADER'S MINDSET

In trading psychology, there are two kinds of trader's mindset. One that fails to seal a deal and one the recovers from failures. There are traders who see failures as just a small setback. And experience where they get to objectify look at what went wrong to avoid similar mistakes to happen again. A winning trader sees these setbacks a part of the steps towards success.

The mindset of a losing trader does not work this way. Success only comes to those who really` really want it. Losing traders tend to not take responsibility for their actions. They tend to blame external factors for their mistakes and losses. In order for a losing trader to become a winner trader, one must take responsibility for his action.

Every successful trader has a dream to succeed. Their thoughts are followed by actions. Losing traders tend to leave their thoughts hanging. They may spend too much of their time talking or visualizing. What is required is action. Traders who think too much tend to look for the perfect opportunity in a trade. What happens is that they also tend to switch or move from one method to another making it difficult for them to find the results that they are looking for.

Traders who think too much, needs to know the effect before they make any decision. Trading is a combination of risk taking and use of a good methodology. This kind of trader looks and demands perfection every time. This compromises their ability to take risks and therefore their ability to trade.

The opposite of thinking traders are those new traders who lack patience and discipline. These types of traders get caught up in their emotions or ideas then they make decisions that they regret in the end. They rush without thinking of the trading plan or method. They are driven by success, but they clearly lack discipline. They completely rely on their instincts. They may go on with a trade thinking that eventually everything will go all right if something does go wrong. Unlike thinking traders, undisciplined traders trade recklessly with their capital.

So, if you think you are on the losing trader's side of the fence, then how do you get to the other side?

What is the thought process running in head of a successful trader?

Will power and discipline are two things that separate a successful trader from the rest. When the trader's confidence is down and shaken, then there will be a bigger problem to resolve and will require extra willpower to finish the job.

Successful traders are not afraid and overcome fear when making decisions. This does not necessarily mean that traders are reckless. One has to take calculated risks. There are also people who trade because they want to achieve their dreams. Successful traders sit down and depend on the plan that they made. A trading plan will make sure that you are following a trading method.

Another key to success is implementing your strict management rules and following them mechanically every day. Traders must be disciplined, stay in control and not let either fear or greed rule them. They must cut losses short, maximize gains and most importantly of all; protect their capital. A losing trader can change their trading mindset for the better. A healthy and a disciplined mindset can be the start of a losing trader's journey to success and high profits.

CHAPTER 8

USEFUL TIPS IN ESTABLISHING YOUR TRADING MINDSET

If you want to succeed at trading always make it a point to decide wisely and here are some useful tips in establishing your trading mindset.

These may be radical tips for the casual reader, but it has helped a lot of hardy and steadfast successful traders make their mark in the trading market.

First tip is not to mix or listen to anyone. The trading market is also one of stiff competition. The success of one result vs the downfall of another.

Trading is like gambling, do not show your cards since those that are in the market will also not lay down their cards for you.

It is a painful truth that 90% of traders lose, so what will it gain for others to make you win?

Second tip, no one else knows better than you.

People tend to get or consult for advice about everything and call for an expert about your car, homemaking or do-it-yourself handiwork, but those are not a competitive or fierce market.

There are trading experts, but trading is a gamble. You know or manage your risks, opportunities and advantages better than others, so rely on your wise and good judgment.

Everywhere there are experts selling systems which have never been traded, new traders buy them and think they're going to get rich, truth is, no one can give you success, you have to work for it and earn it- that's the hard and fast rule for establishing your trading mindset.

In trading you are on your own and you know best.

Make your own trading rules, after all, you are the one who best knows how to play your cards and set it in motion to work profitably for you.

People are used to a structured society, we know what time we need to be at work, not to drop litter in public and to stop at red traffic lights, but the trade market has no rules that will always make you win. It's a dog eat dog atmosphere where if one wins, another should lose.

Your rules apply to you and you can do what you want - no one tells you what to do.

Finally, you must know how to be firm in your decisions. If you may take a decision that would result in losing, don't try to beat yourself up. Learn from where you failed and set it as a benchmark for your trading path and establishing your trading mindset.

This may be a selfish approach towards trading, but this is how it really looks like in the competitive world of the trading market and how to best approach it is your foolhardy resolve to design, plan and map out your moves.

The fact is, trading mindsets have to be completely different than our normal day-to-day mindsets about living and that's why so many traders lose - they can't change.

Try to be different and make the most out of these useful tips in establishing your trading mindset and if you can, enjoy your spectacular trading success.

CHAPTER 9

WEALTH MINDSET-TRADING DETAILS

Trading requires a healthy mindset. Our trading psychology and methodology gives us an edge. Our trading system helps us identify high probability trades, we enter those trades at the right time, protect our capital and let our profits run. With a healthy trading mindset, we implement a system where in we are comfortable using it. We are consistent and disciplined when following our trading plans.

Aside from rigorously following our trade plan, we also void becoming emotional. If it is an emotional day, we do not hasten the pace of our trades. Every trader beginners or advanced make mistakes. We learn from our mistakes and grow from them. By keeping a log of our trades, we get to monitor or learn something from our previous trade experiences. We can monitor our progress even if there is only slow progress.

When we learn how to control our emotional state, we develop a wealth mindset. The Neurolinguistic Programming or NLP is directed into having a wealthy and healthy mindset. Our brain is directed towards making more positive choices. With NLP, we don't conform with the idea that everything is applicable for everybody. So, in achieving a wealth mindset through NLP, it is by practicing the techniques in order to identify what is best and works for you and your needs.

Wealth mindset techniques may be different, but they have commonalities. There are wealth mindset techniques required of 15 to 30 minutes of training and can be used immediately. While there are techniques that are repetitive exercises and can be done weekly. Some are once-only private processes that can later be accessed in any situation.

When choosing a technique, you can experiment to find out what is best for you. Read through the following descriptions of the wealth mindset techniques and you will have an idea if it will work for you. There are different NLP techniques, they are the following:

(1)   _Anchoring_ – a technique by which can be associated with a desired emotion to a particular situation. A trader would be able to benefit by changing any unwanted emotional state in a few moments, like being frustrated over a deal.

(2)   _Rehearsal _ – a technique by which you can train your brain to expect success by rehearsing for it. As a trader, you face different kinds of situations every day. By this technique, you can regularly condition yourself for success.

(3)   _Using a mentor_ – this technique encourages guidance from a mentor. A mentor already has a developed mindset, he is there to answer your questions about strategies and methods. This can be big help especially since you will be able to incorporate your mentor's beliefs, emotions and methods.

(4)   _Physiology_- physiology or body posture can change your state instantly. Maintaining positive state of mind is essential in keeping a wealth mindset. You would be able to change you state at will.

(5)   _Vocabulary_ – this technique utilizes the words you speak and think to change your life. What you say to yourself and to others affects the wealth mindset.

(6)   _Setting goals_- this technique focusses your mind on a specific target. Goal setting is a key component of the wealth mindset. Once the goals have been identified, the subconscious mind will begin scanning for opportunities to attain them.

Once you have tested each wealth tested technique or experimented with them, take note of the techniques that appealed to you. Then set up a time each day when you can use them until they become a habit. This would get you started. This wealth mindset will help you keep on toes when doing your trading.

We hope you have enjoyed reading this book and we wish you all the possible success in your journey as a trader.

THE OTHER SIDE OF WALL STREET

OUR TRADING SYSTEM

Learning our System is easy, both for novices and experienced traders.

We have created a comprehensive training curriculum to ensure that you not only learn the method, but you are successful in applying it. It takes a year of mentoring and practice to develop the level of mastery necessary for sustainable success.

Our System is not a "get rich quick" scheme. With all things truly worthwhile, it takes time and dedication to create your desired results. We at The Other Side of Wall Street are with you **every** step of the way to ensure your success is supported.

OPTIONEERING FOR INCOME

In this 3-day live training course, learn the entire foundation for trading. We will walk you through a step-by-step comprehensive curriculum guaranteed to teach you everything you need to know: non-directional trading mastery; basic technical analysis so you can place solid trades; how to "adjust" if a trade "gets in trouble;" create a personalized trading plan; and master your trading psychology.

PAPER TRADE

Place "practice trades" for 1 year so that you can grow your skills and confidence and get comfortable with the electronic trading platform (thinkorswim). These trades function like live trades, but they are placed with digital (fake) money so that your learning mistakes can never risk real money. This is your apprenticeship year, during which you embody the skills of non-directional trading and master your trading psychology.

WEEKLY Q&A WEBINARS

With your OFI course registration, you receive a bonus 3-month free subscription to the Weekly Q&A Webinars which happen once per week. Will review the market conditions for the week and demonstrate how to best strategize your trades. You will have the opportunity to ask all your questions and receive customized support. The webinars are so valuable our students remain participants for the lifetime of their trading activities.

WEEKLY RADIO SHOW

Join us each week for a half hour of instructional radio where we discuss and teach all the aspects of our trading program.

ADVANCED COURSES

Advanced trading strategies and advanced technical analysis are key to helping you minimize risk and maximize profit. Once you have taken the OFI Course, participated in the Webinars for at least 3 months and successfully Paper Traded for at least 3 months, you are invited to take both of our Advanced Courses (live trainings) in any order: Advanced Optioneering for Income and Advanced Technical Analysis. Up level your trading know-how.

HERE IT IS IN NUTSHELL...

If it sounds complicated, it's really not. Whether you are a novice that has never followed the market in your life, or you have been trading for years and are ready to make more money, our courses and support resources will teach you everything you need to know.

TECHNICAL ANALYSIS

Analyze the Historical Trading Range - all past price movement - high and low prices - of SPX for a maximum of 1 year. Strategically identify the strike prices at which to sell Options - on both sides of the range (selling the Iron Condor).

OPTION SELLING

Establish a Position by selling weekly Options. In case the Option goes In the Money, for protection, buy Options for less premium to fulfill the Options we sold in case they are exercised. Limit risk while maximizing profit.

NON-DIRECTIONAL PROFIT

Profit occurs at the time we sell the Option. When the price stays within the Trading Range that we established with our Position, the Option expires worthless. Because the Option was not exercised, we keep the premium as our profit.

ADJUSTING

If a trade is in danger of breaking through the Trading Range, we "adjust" our position to expire later, moving it out of the way of expiring In the Money this week. We keep our profit. *We the only system that teaches this secret weapon.*

We hope you enjoyed this book and we encourage you to visit us at:

www.theothersideofwallstreet.org

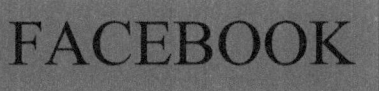

The Other Side
of Wall Street

The Other Side of Wall Street, 1835 Newport Blvd. A109 Suite 652, Costa Mesa, Ca. 92627

(949) 734-1698

info@theothersideofwallstreet.com

© 2019 The Other Side of Wall Street, All Rights Reserved

www.ingramcontent.com/pod-product-compliance
Lightning Source LLC
Chambersburg PA
CBHW031507210526
45463CB00003B/1120